THIS IS A HISTORY OF:

_____

I STARTED THIS JOURNAL ON:

_____

IN THE CITY OF:

_____

I COMPLETED THIS JOURNAL ON:

_____

IN THE CITY OF:

_____

THIS JOURNAL IS ESPECIALLY FOR:

_____

This is my history and it is also your history.

I hope that, as you read it, you will be encouraged to keep a journal

so your children can learn all about you.

A Father's Journal

Memories for my child

by Linda Kranz
photography by Klaus Kranz

NORTHLAND PUBLISHING

More journals by Linda Kranz:

All About Me: A Keepsake Journal for Kids

More About Me: Another Keepsake Journal for Kids

Through My Eyes: A Journal for Teens

For My Child: A Mother's Keepsake Journal

To order, call 1 (800) 346-3257

The text type was set in Golden Cockerel ITC
The display type was set in Janson
Designed by Mike Russell
Art Directed by Jennifer Schaber
Edited by Stephanie Bucholz
Production Supervised by Lisa Brownfield
Composed and manufactured in the United States of America

First Impression
ISBN 0-87358-712-x

0761/7.5M/6-99

For Klaus:

Thank you for more than twenty-five years of understanding my words even before they were spoken; for being an "involved" Dad to our Jessica and Nikolaus; and most of all, for your love: you AMAZE me!

And to all dads:

Encourage your children to do those things in life that bring them the most happiness. Life should be ENJOYED every day!

INTRODUCTION

WHAT DO FATHERS THINK about life, family, and the world around them? A friend said to me, not long ago, "My dad never says much, but I can tell in his eyes, and his smile, that if given the right opportunity, he would offer such a wealth of insight. He is ready to share. He just needs the right vehicle to get him started."

We turn to our fathers for advice, guidance, and love. In their own way, differently than our mothers, they are always there for their children. I want to share with you some comments I received when I told several friends that I was thinking of writing a father's journal.

From Mark, who's in his late thirties: "My father was a farmer. I was the oldest of four children. I rarely had time alone with my dad. I craved to be noticed. Now that I'm a dad, I want to be there for my son. We learn from our childhood experiences, and daily life, how we want to parent. These thoughts should be passed on to our children."

From Greg, who's in his early sixties: "I've had a wonderful life. I've seen places I never dreamt I'd see. I've watched my children grow up and rise above many obstacles. They have made me proud time and time again. I see how the world has changed and I have things I want to tell my family: observations that never seem to come up when we talk. I've been wanting to write down my thoughts for some time, but I didn't know where to begin. With this journal it will be easy."

From Scott, who's in his mid-forties: "My daughter is a teenager. She is independent, which is how I hoped she would be. But she is distant so much of the time. I want to let her know that her safety is my top concern. That setting standards now—like curfews, doing homework before she goes out with her friends—is only in her best interest. Years from now, I hope, she will see why I did these things. In this journal I can write how I'm feeling right now."

A Note About Using This Journal:

Filling up these pages will be a labor of love. It will require you to remember and reflect, to think ahead and to share the unique elements that make you who you are. Take your time. I've heard from so many people that the hardest part seems to be answering the first few questions. After that, the thoughts will flow easily onto the pages.

Read through the questions. Go in any order you like. Once you start, I'm sure these questions will bring up memories unique to your life. Several pages say "Write more memories here." On those pages you can make this journal very personal for your child. If you don't have an answer for my question, write your own.

What a treasure this journal will be when it's completed in your own handwriting. Here's your opportunity to tell your life story in your own words. Don't wait another day; start writing and be remembered!

—LINDA KRANZ

About me

CHILDHOOD MEMORIES.

Where I was born. First friends that I remember. Games I played, favorite stories.

A time I was scared. A time I felt proud.

_____

_____

_____

_____

_____

_____

_____

_____

_____

_____

_____

_____

_____

_____

_____

MEMORIES OF MY SCHOOL DAYS.

The schools I went to. My favorite teachers. Why they made a difference in my life.

Classrooms I can remember.

_____

_____

_____

_____

_____

_____

_____

_____

_____

_____

_____

_____

_____

_____

_____

_____

_____

_____

MY FAVORITE SUBJECT.

The grade or grades I enjoyed most in school, and why. Sports I played.

My saddest memory. My happiest memory.

_____

_____

_____

_____

_____

_____

_____

_____

_____

_____

_____

_____

_____

_____

_____

_____

_____

_____

_____

MEMORIES OF HOUSES I HAVE LIVED IN.

The yards. About our house now. Why we chose this neighborhood over others.

_____

_____

_____

_____

_____

_____

_____

_____

_____

_____

_____

_____

_____

_____

_____

_____

_____

PLACES I HAVE LIVED.

About the city or town I live in now. How I came to live here.

The population. Changes I have seen in the time I have lived here.

_____

_____

_____

_____

_____

_____

_____

_____

_____

_____

_____

_____

_____

_____

_____

_____

_____

_____

_____

_____

_____

_____

WHAT I REMEMBER ABOUT MY TEEN YEARS.

Friends, where we would hang out.

Things I wish I had done. Things I'm glad I did.

MEMORIES OF MY PARENTS WHEN I WAS GROWING UP.

Our daily routine. What we would talk about.

_____

_____

_____

_____

_____

_____

_____

_____

_____

_____

_____

_____

_____

_____

_____

_____

_____

_____

MY FAVORITE HOLIDAY WHEN I WAS GROWING UP.

The memories that come to mind. Traditions in our family now.

_____

_____

_____

_____

_____

_____

_____

_____

_____

_____

_____

_____

_____

_____

_____

_____

_____

_____

_____

_____

_____

_____

Write more memories here.

GIVE COMPLIMENTS AND PRAISE WITH SINCERITY.

NO MATTER HOW OLD THEY ARE, NEVER STOP LETTING YOUR

CHILDREN KNOW HOW PROUD YOU ARE OF THEIR ACCOMPLISHMENTS.

REMIND YOUR CHILD THAT, WITH THE RIGHT ATTITUDE,

AMAZING THINGS CAN HAPPEN.

TEACH YOUR CHILDREN TO BE ORIGINAL THINKERS.

TO BE FLEXIBLE. UNIQUE. AND TO GO AFTER THEIR DREAMS.

HOBBIES I HAVE TAKEN UP OVER THE YEARS.

What got me started. Other hobbies I would like to try.

MY AVERAGE WEEKDAY.

How it starts, develops, and ends. Does it change as the seasons change? The weekend. How it

starts, develops, and ends. What I like to do on the weekends.

_____

_____

_____

_____

_____

_____

_____

_____

_____

_____

_____

_____

_____

_____

_____

_____

_____

_____

MY THOUGHTS ABOUT PETS. PETS I HAD AS A CHILD.

Their names. My memories of them.

THE WEATHER.

What time of the year I like best. Dangerous weather I have seen.

Beautiful sunsets, full moon skies, starry nights.

MY MEMORIES ABOUT HOW I LEARNED TO DRIVE.

My first car. My favorite car was . . .

_____

_____

_____

_____

_____

_____

_____

_____

_____

_____

_____

_____

_____

_____

_____

_____

_____

_____

WHAT I HAVE LEARNED OVER THE

YEARS ABOUT DRIVING.

About cars. Advice I would like to share with you.

MY FIRST JOB.

What it was like. My weekly salary. Other jobs I have had. Why I chose my profession.

How I feel about it.

Antonio's Pizza
DELIVERY
GUS

_____

_____

_____

_____

_____

_____

_____

_____

_____

_____

_____

_____

_____

_____

_____

_____

_____

_____

_____

_____

_____

_____

_____

"I'M QUITE HAPPY WHERE I AM . . ." OR

"IF I COULD CHANGE MY CAREER, THIS IS WHAT I WOULD DO . . ."

Suggestions about choosing a career. Hints for working side by side with coworkers.

_____

_____

_____

_____

_____

_____

_____

_____

_____

_____

_____

_____

_____

_____

_____

_____

_____

_____

_____

_____

_____

Write more memories here.

WHETHER IT BE NATURE, SPORTS, BOOKS, OR WORLD MATTERS,
FIND LIKE "LOVES" AND HAVE
LONG CONVERSATIONS WITH YOUR CHILD.

ENCOURAGE LAUGHTER. BE SPONTANEOUS.

SET ASIDE TIME EXCLUSIVELY FOR YOU AND YOUR CHILD TO
SPEND TOGETHER, REGULARLY. THIS ROUTINE WILL SURELY BE
THE BRIGHT SPOT OF YOUR WEEK.

HOW I LIKE TO SPEND MY TIME IN THE EVENINGS.

Ways I like to unwind.

_____

_____

_____

_____

_____

_____

_____

_____

_____

_____

_____

_____

_____

_____

_____

_____

_____

_____

_____

MY FAVORITE MOVIES, ACTORS . . .

Why I enjoy them.

_____

_____

_____

_____

_____

_____

_____

_____

THE KIND OF MUSIC THAT WAS PLAYED IN OUR HOUSE WHEN I WAS YOUNG.

The kind of music I listen to now.

_____

_____

_____

_____

_____

_____

_____

_____

FRIENDS.

How we met. How we've managed to stay in touch over the years.

What it means to be a friend.

_____

_____

_____

_____

_____

_____

_____

_____

_____

_____

_____

_____

_____

_____

_____

_____

_____

_____

THE EMOTIONS I FELT WHEN WE DISCOVERED

WE WERE GOING TO HAVE A CHILD.

The first people we told.

_____

_____

_____

_____

_____

_____

_____

_____

_____

MY THOUGHTS AND FEELINGS WHEN I SAW YOU FOR THE FIRST TIME.

What I remember about that day. How we decided on your name.

_____

_____

_____

_____

_____

_____

_____

_____

_____

WHAT I HAVE DONE DIFFERENTLY WITH MY OWN FAMILY.

What my parents did when they raised me.

THINGS THAT ARE IMPORTANT TO ME.

(Make a list and keep adding to it.)

Write more memories here.

REMEMBER THEIR SMILE, THEIR LAUGHTER, THEIR EXPRESSIONS
WHEN THEY ACCOMPLISHED SOMETHING FOR THE FIRST TIME.
RECALLING THOSE MEMORIES WILL WARM YOU
FROM THE INSIDE OUT.

TEACH YOUR CHILDREN TO BE INDEPENDENT. BUT ALWAYS BE
AVAILABLE IN CASE THEY NEED YOUR HELP.

ENCOURAGE; DON'T CRITICIZE.

WHAT I THINK THE FUTURE WILL BE LIKE.

The changes I would like to see. I hope that in your lifetime . . .

_____

_____

_____

_____

_____

_____

_____

_____

_____

_____

_____

_____

_____

_____

_____

_____

_____

_____

_____

_____

_____

_____

LOCAL OR GLOBAL NEWS EVENTS THAT I HAVE FOLLOWED
WITH GREAT INTEREST OVER THE COURSE OF MY LIFE.

Why they caught my attention.

_____

_____

_____

_____

_____

_____

_____

_____

_____

_____

_____

_____

_____

_____

_____

_____

_____

_____

_____

_____

How I met your mother.

What interested me in her. How old we were. How long we dated.

What I know about her now that I didn't know on our wedding day.

_____

_____

_____

_____

_____

_____

_____

_____

_____

_____

_____

_____

_____

_____

_____

_____

_____

_____

MEMORIES OF OUR WEDDING DAY.

Where we were married. Where we went on our honeymoon and what it was like.

MEMORIES OF OUR FIRST HOME.

How was it furnished? The view we could see out of our living room window.

How long we lived there.

_____

_____

_____

_____

_____

_____

_____

_____

_____

_____

_____

_____

_____

_____

_____

_____

_____

_____

_____

_____

_____

_____

_____

IF I HAD TO DESCRIBE A FEW OF MY HAPPIEST MEMORIES,

these are the ones that quickly come to mind.

VACATIONS I REMEMBER GOING ON AS A CHILD

and through the years.

_____

_____

_____

_____

_____

_____

_____

_____

_____

_____

_____

_____

_____

_____

_____

_____

_____

_____

_____

_____

THE NICEST THING I EVER DID FOR MY MOM AND DAD.

_____

_____

_____

_____

_____

_____

_____

_____

_____

_____

_____

_____

_____

_____

_____

_____

_____

_____

_____

_____

HOW I WOULD DESCRIBE MYSELF AS A PERSON.

My likes and dislikes, habits, qualities, ways my temperament has changed over the years.

_____

_____

_____

_____

_____

_____

_____

_____

_____

_____

_____

_____

_____

_____

_____

_____

_____

Write more memories here.

POINT OUT BEAUTIFUL THINGS TO YOUR CHILDREN SO THEY
WILL LEARN TO LOOK FOR GOOD THINGS ON THEIR OWN.

NEVER BE TOO BUSY TO STOP AND LISTEN TO YOUR CHILD.

ENCOURAGE YOUR CHILD TO SET GOALS.
WHEN THEY HAVE MET A GOAL, THEY SHOULD SET ANOTHER
AND ANOTHER, AND SO ON. BY DOING THIS THEY WILL GO FAR.

THINGS I WOULD DO DIFFERENTLY IF I WERE TO HAVE ANOTHER CHILD.

Things I would relax about. Things I would notice more.

_____

_____

_____

_____

_____

_____

_____

_____

_____

_____

_____

_____

_____

_____

_____

_____

_____

_____

_____

_____

_____

_____

WAYS YOUR MOTHER HAS SURPRISED ME OVER THE YEARS.

Ways I have surprised her.

_____

_____

_____

_____

_____

_____

_____

_____

_____

_____

_____

_____

_____

_____

_____

_____

_____

_____

PLACES I HAVE VISITED THAT I WANT TO TELL YOU ABOUT.

My memories of those places and what I liked or disliked about them.

Thoughts on traveling.

_____

_____

_____

_____

_____

_____

_____

_____

_____

_____

_____

_____

_____

_____

_____

_____

_____

_____

_____

THINGS I'VE DONE THAT HAVE TAKEN ME OUT OF MY COMFORT ZONE.

How it felt to take risks. How those things turned out.

ACCOMPLISHMENTS IN MY LIFE THAT I AM PROUD OF.

Goals that I am working on now.

_____

_____

_____

_____

_____

_____

_____

_____

_____

_____

_____

_____

_____

_____

_____

_____

_____

_____

_____

_____

MY "I WOULD LOVE TO HAVE" LIST.

Things I don't necessarily need, but would enjoy having.

_____

_____

_____

_____

_____

_____

_____

_____

_____

_____

_____

_____

_____

_____

_____

_____

_____

_____

_____

_____

TOYS I REMEMBER FROM MY CHILDHOOD.

_____
_____
_____
_____
_____
_____
_____
_____
_____
_____
_____
_____
_____
_____
_____
_____
_____
_____
_____
_____
_____
_____
_____

If I could travel anywhere in the world, it would be . . .

Why I want to go there.

_____

_____

_____

_____

_____

_____

_____

_____

_____

_____

_____

_____

_____

_____

_____

_____

_____

_____

_____

_____

_____

_____

_____

IF SOMEONE GAVE ME A MILLION DOLLARS,

no strings attached, this is what I would do.

_____

_____

_____

_____

_____

_____

_____

_____

_____

_____

_____

_____

_____

_____

_____

_____

_____

_____

_____

_____

_____

_____

_____

If i could live anywhere i wanted, i would choose . . .

Write more memories here.

_____

WHEN WAS THE LAST TIME YOU SAID "I LOVE YOU"
_____
TO YOUR CHILDREN?
_____
TELL THEM OFTEN SO THEY WILL KNOW THAT IT IS TRUE.
_____

_____

_____

IF YOU GIVE YOUR WORD, STICK TO IT!
_____
YOUR CHILD WILL FOLLOW YOUR EXAMPLE.
_____

_____

_____

INVOLVE YOUR CHILD IN DECISION MAKING.
_____
EXPLAIN YOUR DECISIONS.
_____

_____

_____

_____

_____

_____

If I had to name a few things my parents taught me they would be . . .

_____

_____

_____

_____

_____

_____

_____

_____

I hope that, when my children are grown, they will say they learned this from me . . .

_____

_____

_____

_____

_____

_____

_____

_____

NOW THAT I'M ____ YEARS OLD,

these are the things that I've learned about life, love, family, friends. (Keep adding to this list.)

TRACE AROUND YOUR HAND AND WRITE THE DATE.

Your child will cherish this page and will enjoy placing his or her hand on yours.

HOW MY PARENTS MAKE/MADE A LIVING.

Memories of their jobs.

WHEN I'M GONE, I WANT TO BE REMEMBERED THIS WAY . . .

If I had to describe the most challenging part of being a parent, I would say . . .

_____

_____

_____

_____

_____

_____

_____

_____

_____

_____

_____

_____

_____

_____

_____

_____

_____

_____

_____

_____

_____

If I had to describe the most rewarding part of being a parent, I would say . . .

_____

_____

_____

_____

_____

_____

_____

_____

_____

_____

_____

_____

_____

_____

_____

_____

_____

_____

_____

MY FAVORITE BOOKS THROUGH THE YEARS.

Favorite authors.

_____
_____
_____
_____
_____
_____
_____
_____
_____
_____
_____
_____
_____
_____
_____
_____
_____
_____
                    _____
                    _____
                    _____
                    _____
                    _____
                    _____

Write more memories here.

IF THEY SAY "BUT IT'S ALREADY BEEN DONE," TELL THEM TO

THINK OF A NEW WAY, A BETTER WAY,

AND THEIR IDEA JUST MIGHT CATCH ON.

ENCOURAGE CREATIVITY.

TALK ABOUT YOUR DREAMS.

SHARE THEM WITH YOUR CHILDREN,

AND THEY WILL CERTAINLY SHARE

SOME OF THEIR DREAMS WITH YOU.

EVERY CHILD NEEDS HIS OR HER OWN SPACE.

HONOR IT. ALLOW IT. ENCOURAGE IT.

KNOCK BEFORE ENTERING YOUR CHILD'S ROOM.

HOW TECHNOLOGY HAS CHANGED SINCE I WAS YOUNG.

Things you take for granted that I never had.

HOW PRICES HAVE CHANGED OVER THE YEARS.

The cost of gas. A haircut. A first class postage stamp. A visit to the doctor.

Utility bills. House payments.

ABOUT MY FAMILY.

How I got along with my sisters and brothers. How many years between us.

A memory that stands out about each of my siblings.

_____

_____

_____

_____

_____

_____

_____

_____

_____

_____

_____

_____

_____

_____

_____

_____

_____

_____

_____

_____

SIBLINGS.

How our relationships have changed, now that we are adults.

Or thoughts on being an only child.

_____

_____

_____

_____

_____

_____

_____

_____

_____

_____

_____

_____

_____

_____

_____

_____

_____

_____

_____

_____

_____

_____

MEMORIES OF MY FIRST FATHER'S DAY.

Other Father's Days that I especially remember.

WHEN I WAS YOUNG, MORE THAN
ANYTHING I USED TO WISH FOR . . .

MY DESCRIPTION OF SUCCESS, AND SOME EXAMPLES I HAVE SEEN.

EVERYONE IS CONSIDERED EITHER AN INTROVERT

OR AN EXTROVERT, OR HAS SHADES OF BOTH.

This is how I see myself.

TIMES IN MY LIFE THAT I WAS TRULY MOVED.

COINCIDENCES THAT I HAVE NOTICED AT DIFFERENT TIMES IN MY LIFE.

How I feel about this statement: "Everything happens for a reason."

_____

_____

_____

_____

_____

_____

_____

_____

_____

_____

_____

_____

_____

_____

_____

_____

_____

_____

A TIME WHEN I LOST SOMEONE CLOSE TO ME.

How I dealt with those emotions. How I remember that person now.

PEOPLE I ADMIRE AND WHY.

Mentors I had at different times in my life.

_____

_____

_____

_____

_____

_____

_____

_____

_____

_____

_____

_____

_____

_____

_____

_____

_____

_____

Write more memories here.

LET YOUR CHILDREN EXPRESS THEMSELVES IN THEIR OWN WAY.
DON'T INTERRUPT. BE PATIENT.

AS PARENTS, WE SEE TALENTS IN OUR CHILDREN THAT THEY AREN'T
ALWAYS AWARE OF. POINT THEM OUT AND ENCOURAGE YOUR CHILDREN
TO DEVELOP THEM OVER TIME. THEY WILL THANK YOU.

STUDIES ARE ESSENTIAL, BUT SO ARE FRIENDSHIP AND FAMILY TIME.
TEACH YOUR CHILDREN HOW TO BALANCE THESE THINGS.

The best thing about getting older.

_____

_____

_____

_____

_____

_____

_____

_____

_____

_____

_____

_____

_____

The worst thing about getting older.

_____

_____

_____

_____

_____

_____

When I think about my dad, these words and memories come to mind.

_____

_____

_____

_____

_____

_____

_____

_____

_____

_____

_____

_____

_____

_____

_____

_____

_____

_____

_____

If I were to consider all the birthdays that I have celebrated,

these are the ones that stand out in my memory:

_____

_____

_____

_____

_____

_____

_____

_____

_____

_____

_____

_____

_____

_____

_____

_____

_____

_____

_____

_____

When I think about my mom, these words and memories come to mind.

_____
_____
_____
_____
_____
_____
_____
_____
_____
_____
_____
_____
_____
_____
_____
_____
_____
_____
_____
_____

A LIST OF THINGS I WANT TO DO

before I can't do them anymore.

SOME QUOTES THAT HAVE INSPIRED ME,

THAT HAVE STAYED WITH ME OVER THE YEARS.

My own quotes.

Some pieces of advice I have received from family and friends
that I'm glad I took to heart.

_____

_____

_____

_____

_____

_____

_____

_____

_____

_____

_____

_____

_____

_____

_____

_____

_____

_____

_____

Write more memories here.

TEACH YOUR CHILDREN TO LOOK FOR THE GOOD IN ALL PEOPLE.

TIME—FROM THE DAY YOUR CHILD IS BORN, UNTIL THE DAY HE OR SHE VENTURES OUT INTO THE WORLD—WILL GO BY SO QUICKLY. MAKE EVERY DAY COUNT!

THERE ARE NO GUARANTEES IN LIFE, AND NO WAY TO KNOW HOW MUCH TIME WE HAVE. SO, WE NEED TO LEARN, TEACH, HAVE FUN, LAUGH, AND LOVE, EACH AND EVERY DAY! NO REGRETS!

Some of my most prized possessions and why they mean so much to me.

Trends I've seen come and go. Trends that are coming back.

ADVICE ON WAYS TO KEEP A LOVE RELATIONSHIP
STRONG AND LONG LASTING.

Just because!

A TIME WHEN I OFFERED MY HELP TO SOMEONE IN NEED.

A time when someone came to my aid.

THINGS I'M THANKFUL FOR . . .

ROUGH TIMES I'VE EXPERIENCED. HOW I MADE IT THROUGH THEM.

What kept me going.

FAMILY STORIES I WANT YOU TO KNOW ABOUT.

FINANCES.

Sticking to budgets. Setting money aside for a rainy day. Some suggestions.

Write more memories here.

_____

YOUR CHILDREN WATCH YOU SO CLOSELY. THEY WATCH HOW
YOU REACT TO EVERY SITUATION.

_____

_____

_____

_____

YOUR EXPRESSIONS MIRROR YOUR FEELINGS. BY WATCHING YOU
THEY LEARN HOW TO LOVE.

_____

_____

_____

_____

WHEN YOUR CHILD CAN NO LONGER CALL YOU ON THE PHONE TO
ASK YOU QUESTIONS, ADVICE, OR JUST TO TALK,
THIS COMPLETED JOURNAL WILL BE A MOST TREASURED KEEPSAKE.

_____

_____

_____

Events in my life that, given a second chance, I would change

how I approached them the first time.

If I had two extra hours each day to spend any way I wanted,

this is what I would do:

_____

_____

_____

_____

_____

_____

_____

_____

_____

_____

_____

_____

_____

_____

_____

_____

_____

_____

_____

_____

_____

_____

_____

_____

_____

_____

_____

_____

_____

_____

_____

_____

_____

_____

_____

_____

_____

_____

_____

_____

_____

_____

SOME WORDS OF WISDOM AND ADVICE I WOULD LIKE TO LEAVE

for my children, grandchildren, and those that come after them.

_____

_____

_____

_____

_____

_____

_____

_____

_____

_____

_____

_____

_____

_____

_____

_____

_____

_____

_____

_____

_____

_____

About you

WHAT MADE YOU A SPECIAL CHILD.

Some of your best qualities.

THINGS YOU DID THAT MADE ME PROUD.

WHAT I REMEMBER ABOUT YOUR FIRST DAY OF SCHOOL.

Special teachers you had that made a difference in your life.

WAYS I FOUND TO BE INVOLVED WITH YOUR HOMEWORK

AND OTHER SCHOOL ACTIVITIES.

How you took to school.

_____

_____

_____

_____

_____

_____

_____

_____

_____

_____

_____

_____

_____

_____

_____

_____

_____

_____

Report card		1	2
Name Jessica		A	A
Reading			
Effort			
Skills			
Comprehension			
Independent Reading	A		
Language Usage			
Effort			
Oral Expression			
Written Expression			
Grammar-Punctuation			
Spelling			
Effort			
Applies correct spelling in written work			
Learns assigned words			
Mathematics			
Effort			
Concepts			
Basic Skills			
Problem Solving			

TIMES YOU WERE AFRAID.

How your mother and I dealt with those times.

_____

_____

_____

_____

_____

_____

_____

_____

_____

_____

_____

_____

_____

_____

_____

_____

_____

_____

_____

_____

_____

_____

HOLIDAY MEMORIES THAT ARE STILL AS
CLEAR AS IF THEY HAPPENED YESTERDAY.

_____

_____

_____

_____

_____

_____

_____

_____

_____

_____

_____

_____

_____

_____

_____

_____

_____

_____

_____

_____

BOOKS YOU LOVED THROUGH THE YEARS.

SIBLINGS.

Ways you would interact. Or thoughts on being an only child.

LITTLE WAYS YOU SHOWED ME THAT YOU LOVED ME.

TIMES WHEN I SURPRISED YOU.

Your reactions.

_____

_____

_____

_____

_____

_____

_____

_____

_____

_____

_____

_____

_____

_____

_____

_____

_____

_____

Write more memories here.

When our children go out on their own, we hope they are successful on the path they have chosen. Parenting is a lifelong adventure.

Take time to read a story to your child. Go for a walk in the park. Make time to be together.

Having children makes you appreciate your own parents even more. When your patience is wearing thin, remember that your children will one day be thankful for everything you've done for them.

When I think back to some of your "firsts," these things come to mind.

_____
_____
_____
_____
_____
_____
_____
_____
_____
_____
_____
_____
_____
_____
_____
_____
_____
_____
_____
_____
_____
_____
_____
_____

YOUR ROOM.

How you liked to keep it.

YOUR BIRTHDAYS.

How we celebrated them. Those that I particularly remember.

_____
_____
_____
_____
_____
_____
_____
_____
_____
_____
_____
_____
_____
_____
_____
_____
_____
_____
_____
_____
_____
_____

PETS.

What they have meant to you over the years.

_____

_____

_____

_____

_____

_____

_____

_____

_____

_____

_____

_____

_____

_____

_____

_____

_____

_____

_____

Write more memories here.

_____

_____

GIVEN THE RIGHT TOOLS EARLY IN LIFE,
CHILDREN WILL BE WELL EQUIPPED FOR LIFE AND WILL
EVENTUALLY SHARE THOSE TOOLS WITH THEIR OWN CHILDREN.
THEY WILL REMEMBER.

_____

_____

_____

REMEMBER BACK TO YOUR OWN CHILDHOOD FROM TIME
TO TIME. THIS WILL HELP YOU SEE FROM YOUR CHILD'S EYES
WHERE HE OR SHE IS COMING FROM.

_____

_____

_____

DON'T COMPARE YOUR CHILDREN TO EACH OTHER.
REALIZE THEY WON'T BE THE SAME WHEN IT COMES TO
STUDIES, PERSONALITY, AND OUTLOOK ON LIFE.
LET THEM BE THEMSELVES.

If I had to write down ten words that describe you, they would be:

You showed your independence by . . .

TIMES WHEN I WANTED TO SPEAK UP IN A
CERTAIN SITUATION, YET I HELD BACK.
In hindsight I wish I had . . .

WHAT YOU LIKED TO DO AS THE SEASONS CHANGED.

How you kept busy: winter, spring, summer, and fall.

_____

_____

_____

_____

_____

_____

_____

_____

_____

_____

_____

_____

_____

_____

_____

_____

_____

_____

_____

Toys you could not part with. Where those toys are now.

_____

_____

_____

_____

_____

_____

_____

_____

_____

_____

_____

_____

_____

_____

_____

_____

_____

_____

Write more memories here.

TEACH YOUR CHILDREN HOW TO TAKE CARE OF THEIR ROOMS,
TO COOK, TO BE RESPONSIBLE, TO BALANCE A CHECKBOOK.
TEACH THEM THINGS THEY WILL NEED TO KNOW WHEN THEY
ARE ON THEIR OWN AND THEY WILL FLOURISH.

TAKE LOTS OF PHOTOS. YOUR CHILDREN WILL GROW UP SO FAST!

TEACH YOUR CHILDREN KINDNESS.

Presents you made or bought for me over the years.

Things you said that touched me or made me laugh.

Write more memories here.

THERE WILL COME A TIME WHEN YOUR CHILDREN WILL HAVE
TO TRY THINGS ON THEIR OWN. STEP ASIDE AND TRUST THAT
THEY WILL BE FINE. LET GO.

"IF I ONLY HAD MORE TIME I WOULD . . ."
WHEN YOU CATCH YOURSELF SAYING THIS, REEVALUATE YOUR
PRIORITIES AND MAKE TIME FOR THE MOST IMPORTANT
ASPECTS OF YOUR LIFE.

EMPOWER YOUR CHILDREN ALWAYS TO DO THEIR BEST . . .
AND THEN SOME!

AS PARENTS WE ARE OUR CHILDREN'S TEACHERS.

Yet, I must say you have taught me a thing or two over the years. For instance:

_____   _____

_____   _____

_____   _____

_____   _____

_____

_____

_____

_____

_____

_____

_____

_____

_____

_____

_____

_____

_____

_____

_____

_____

_____

_____